TRUE WEALTH
LEVERAGE NATURAL LAWS
FOR PERPETUAL ABUNDANCE

NGHIEP (NIP) NGUYEN

outskirts
press

True Wealth
Leverage Natural Laws for Perpetual Abundance
All Rights Reserved.
Copyright © 2021 Nghiep (Nip) Nguyen
v3.0

The opinions expressed in this manuscript are solely the opinions of the author and do not represent the opinions or thoughts of the publisher. The author has represented and warranted full ownership and/or legal right to publish all the materials in this book.

This book may not be reproduced, transmitted, or stored in whole or in part by any means, including graphic, electronic, or mechanical without the express written consent of the publisher except in the case of brief quotations embodied in critical articles and reviews.

Outskirts Press, Inc.
http://www.outskirtspress.com

ISBN: 978-1-9772-4339-3

Cover Photo © 2021 www.gettyimages.com. All rights reserved - used with permission.

Outskirts Press and the "OP" logo are trademarks belonging to Outskirts Press, Inc.

PRINTED IN THE UNITED STATES OF AMERICA

Natural laws identify the true source of money and empower us to best exploit this source.

Thanks...

Lana Nguyen and Michelle Vo for the illustrations. Your patience is admired.

Nguyen Thuy for the final touches on the author's photo.

The attendees of the finance seminars at Hiep Luc Community Center in Houston from 2013 to 2018 for consistent attendance, and feedback offering some insights to the class materials as well as the contents of this book.

Tinamarie Ruvalcaba and Elaine Simpson of Outskirts Press, for patiently dealing with all the tedious details during the production process of this book.

Sam Duong Nguyen, my life partner, for loving support and source of inspiration.

I deeply appreciate all of you.

Table of Contents

Preface i

1. The Source of Money 1
2. Who We Really Are? 11
3. Setting and Achieving Goals 31
4. Using Natural Talents 44
5. Becoming an Expert 53
6. Creative Ideas 63

Conclusion: Abundance and Fulfillment 77

Preface

A truly wealthy person and the power of natural laws

We want money, as much as possible. However, having a lot of money, we are still poor or wealthy, depending on how we earn and spend it.

How do we earn money?

Richness means abundance, having the means to buy anything we need. Money is just one of these means. But money is not the ultimate goal.

Pursuing money as the ultimate goal, some people will do anything, even illegal or immoral. They will step on others if necessary. Earning this way, even a lot, we are still "poor." Wealthy people earn money by providing a useful service to others.

If in the process, wealthy people also help all related people earn and eventually become wealthy too, they are truly wealthy people.

How do people spend?

Some people spend lavishly, showing off their wealth while people around them struggle to put food on the table. Should they be proud of having a lot of money? No, there is nothing to be proud of. Such pride is a sign of "poverty."

Truly wealthy people spend just enough to satisfy their needs, using their extra wealth to help less fortunate people to have better lives. Earning a lot empowers them to do meaningful activities. They are not proud of their wealth but happy to have abundant means to help others. They deserve their abundance and feel genuinely happy.

Truly wealthy people know their lives have a divine purpose and are fulfilling it. Their wealth is the result of pursuing this purpose, rendering some profoundly useful service to the community. Then, whatever comes and goes around them, including wealth, does not matter. They feel genuinely satisfied and fulfilled.

So, truly wealthy people earn abundance, feel deserving, happy, and fulfilled.

However, poverty is still a world problem! In October 2020, about 689 million people, or 9.20% of the world population, live in extreme poverty. They earn less than $1.90 a day, according to the World Bank. Many people around the world, in less developed and developed countries alike, are struggling daily to earn a decent living.

This book aims to alleviate the world poverty and assist a person to become truly wealthy.

How?

Leveraging the power of natural laws, we can get what we want. Everything happening around us and in the universe is controlled by natural laws. The earth, so heavy an object, leaning on nothing, has floated around the sun for billions of years. The power of a natural law is behind it. Empty-handed Mahatma Gandhi of India mobilized two hundred million Indians to defeat the fully armed British army to liberate his country because he leveraged the natural power of mob psychology.

Earning money is both difficult and easy. When we do not comply with related natural laws, our tasks become difficult and fail. Complying with natural laws, our tasks become easy and succeed.

Yet, natural laws unveil themselves around us in everything. If we greet people we meet with a cheerful attitude and loving kindness, they tend to treat us with the same attitude: this is a natural law. A flower blooms, a wind blows and shakes a tree's foliage, seasons repeat one after another every year, all manifest according to the power of natural laws, with no exception. Just pay attention; we will perceive nature's power and apply it to render our daily activities easier and more successful.

We identify five natural laws for creating abundance. A natural law supports each chapter.

Chapter one identifies the source of money based on the law of "giving and receiving." Basically, if we provide a useful service to others, we earn money. In addition, the better the service (i.e., more quantity and more quality) we provide, the higher the amount we earn. Hence, besides educating ourselves to provide a useful service, we have to find ways to improve our ability to serve.

Chapter two discovers who we really are and serves as the foundation of the book.

Chapter three shows how the power of the subconscious ensures us to achieve a financial goal.

Chapter four shows how natural talents help to turn a vocation into a vacation. The more we enjoy our work, the more we produce.

Chapter five shows how the compound effect helps us to become top expert in our occupation in a short time.

Finally, chapter six demonstrates how the law of attraction helps obtaining creative ideas, which can revolutionize our productivity.

1

The Source of Money

We all need to earn money for a decent living.

Based on the natural law "to give to receive", we earn money when satisfying a need of the community. In other words, if we do something useful for society, we will earn money. We create value. Creating value for others is the source of money.

Consider an employee of a fast-food restaurant. Cleaning around, cooking in the kitchen, or waiting on customers at the cash register, he helps the restaurant and earns about $10 an hour.

A community has many needs: food, clothing, housing, transportation, health, education, safety, relationships, etc. We are born with physical strength and mental ability that we can develop continuously to be more skilled, more knowledgeable, and more experienced to satisfy a specific need of the community.

At an intersection of Houston under a hot summer, a homeless woman held a sign: "Single mom, stranded, hungry, please help!" Her begging eyes looked at each driver. Her messy hair soaked with sweat rolling down her cheeks, dropping to her dirty shirt, combined with her worn out shoes, all show that her need was real.

People felt sorry for her. Somehow in her life, she did not acquire knowledge and skills to serve for earning a decent living or did not have a chance to serve!

We need education for an intended career. We must become a contributor to our community. Whoever we want to become, whatever career we plan, we must prepare. The more skilled, the more knowledgeable in a field of specialization, the more we can serve and the more we can earn.

If we have no skills and provide no useful service, we earn nothing.

A useful service benefits both the provider and the provided person. Suppose a secretary earns $40 an hour and needs a babysitter for her child. If a person asks for $15 an hour for babysitting, both the secretary and the babysitter are better off. The babysitter earns $15 an hour instead or nothing staying at home watching TV, the secretary still has $25 after paying the babysitter from an hour's work. Both benefit.

We must work on ourselves to acquire the ability to serve. However, when we have the ability to provide a service, we still need to reach people needing our service.

Many people in the community are always busy working but earning no money because they provide no useful service to anyone. They have knowledge and skills to satisfy a need, but whoever they contact does not have that need.

Network marketing is a form of doing business where a network marketer brings a product or service directly from the producer to the consumer, bypassing all middlepersons. It saves money and is a legitimate form of doing business. However, many network marketers do not earn good money because the end-users do not realize their needs. We have the experience of being called by telemarketers or network marketers when we are in the middle of a dinner or enjoying a TV show. We feel irritated and do not want to be bothered. Network marketers may have good products and work hard, but most do not earn enough to justify their efforts.

An experienced network marketer builds a customer base from a "warm market" (consisting of close friends or acquaintances who trust him). His warm market must realize their need for the product or service, first. A few network marketers succeed in letting their warm market convince themselves they need the product. They earn good money.

Similarly, spiritual materials are abundant, but people do not bother reading. Some devoted religious persons standing at busy city intersections, shouting spiritual values to people walking by, but few people stop to listen. These devotees have valuable ideas to offer, but people in a hurry to their daily business do not have the need for spiritual materials offered.

Singer Madonna identifies fans' needs and satisfied them. She earned abundantly. According to *Forbes*, Madonna's estimated net worth in 2019 was $570 million. She identified early key trends in music, style, and popular culture, then incorporated them into her own image and products. She leveraged people's interests, even controversial issues, and sex in particular, to maintain media and public interest. "The Material Girl "sold more than 300 million albums and her tours grossed over $1 billion. Not many singers are in the same sphere as hers.

Remember this:

To earn money, we must provide a useful service to others. It means to find out a need of people and satisfy it.

Money—like happiness—can't be obtained if directly sought after. It's the result of providing a useful service

We are interdependent in society. If everyone perceives one another as brothers and sisters in one family and each person contributes to the common livelihood, then a prosperous life will be guaranteed for every member in the "mega-social family."

If we are self-employed, we must identify the pressing need of our customers and find the best way to satisfy it. If we are not self-employed, we must get a job and keep it.

The secret to getting a job is a wholehearted willingness to serve. Before entering into a job interview, we have to think hard about what we can do to satisfy a need of the company—what knowledge and skills we can offer to help the company, not whether the company can give us an opportunity to earn some money!

Once hired, the way to keep a job is to have a genuine concern about serving others. Do not complain about the difficulty of your job. Just do whatever the company needs, and whatever we can do to help, even beyond requirements and expectations. All companies need people with that working mentality.

In Nashville, Tennessee, a waitress arrives to work on time and often stays past her working shift to finish her work. She happily dedicates herself to serving customers and taking care of the restaurant's needs and interests. In difficult times, when the restaurant struggles to keep business, other employees get laid off. Yet the owner is determined to keep her because the restaurant needs people like her to survive difficult times.

An owner of a car-repair shop in Houston, Texas, is always cheerful to his customers. He does not charge for minor jobs such as inflating a tire or checking and realizing no repair is needed. This owner charges reasonably and gives no absurd diagnosis to extort money from customers. Good words spread around, and his shop is always busy. His attitude displays heartfelt, dedicated service and genuine concern without targeting the customer's wallet.

Focusing on the customer's interests, we feel good about our service. If the purpose of performing a job task is solely monetary gain, earning money will be difficult.

Although the principle of providing a useful service confirms the true source of money, it does not explain why wages differ greatly between people in a community. Why do some people earn about ten dollars an hour while others earn hundreds, or even hundreds of thousands of dollars an hour?

The marginal principle in Economics

A psychological law governs each person's decision-making process: "When someone must choose between two bad decisions, they will choose the less harmful one. Likewise, when choosing between two beneficial decisions, they will take the more beneficial one."

This rule, referred to as the marginal principle, explains the difference in wages and provides a rationality to increase income.

Suppose we are the owner of a company and need to decide on the salary for a future employee we plan to hire. If this future employee can help our company's profits to increase by $20,000 a year, we can pay him less than $20,000 a year. If we know this employee can help increasing the company's profits by $500,000 a year, we can pay him any amount up to but less than $500,000.

If we provide greater service (i.e., better quality and more quantity) for the company, we earn more money. There is no limit! So, we must continuously work on ourselves to increase our ability to serve.

A need for a product/service is pressing if:

- many people need it,

- the need is urgent and/or fulfilling that need brings tremendous pleasure,

- the price of similar product/service is higher, and

- the number of people satisfying that need is small.

Many people needed a personal computer in the mid of 1970s and Bill Gates rode that megatrend to great wealth. Getting relevant information coming from anywhere in the world brings tremendous pleasure, especially when we can get it in a few seconds. Google satisfies this need, and its founders legitimately made a fortune. Similarly, the founders of YouTube have satisfied the need to share videos with people around the world and legitimately made a fortune.

The Source of Money

In 2020, the need to find a vaccine for Covid 19 was urgent for people/governments all over the world. But just a few companies—starting with Pfizer and Moderna, then Johnson & Johnson and AstraZeneca—succeeded in producing it. If the governments do not pay for the vaccination, people who can afford it will still pay any price for it.

How can one have resources to satisfy a need of the community?

Nature is amazing! Nature equips us with an inherent ability to survive. At least, Nature gives us a physical body and a functional mind, with which we can do something to earn a decent living.

In addition, each community has plenty of resources for us to take advantage of to grow personally. Whatever occupation we want to specialize in, whatever career we want to pursue, we have schools, universities, and seminars to make progress in that occupation and to grow in our career.

If we take time to develop the physical body and the mind, we can advance our abilities beyond any boundaries.

Born black in the USA in the latter part of the 20th century was a disadvantage; being black and female furthered that disadvantage. However, Oprah Winfrey started from both disadvantages to great success. She was born in the rural town of Kosciusko, Mississippi, on January 29, 1954. After a troubled adolescence in a small farming community, where she was sexually abused by a few male relatives and friends of her mother, she moved to Nashville, Tennessee to live with her father.

Winfrey entered Tennessee State University and began working in radio and television broadcasting in Nashville. She kept developing herself as a talk-show host, media executive, actress, and billionaire philanthropist. She was best known for being the host of her own, famous popular program, *The Oprah Winfrey Show*, which aired for 25 seasons, from 1986 to 2011. In 2011, Winfrey launched her own TV network, the Oprah Winfrey Network (OWN). As of 2020, Oprah is a billionaire.

"But," you say, "Oprah is special!" Yes, she is special because she keeps developing her potential for greatness. But each of us has the same potential, which we must develop. We are all equal and the difference is whether we develop this potential within.

Hence, develop our inner potential, learn specialized knowledge, and create value for others, then EARN!

The next chapter is about that inner potential everyone has.

2

Who We Really Are?

The search for our true nature

A lady lost her husband due to a heart attack. He was the family's breadwinner, and she had no choice but to move her five young children to live under a bridge in the city. She visualized her family's future and felt hopeless and scared. A man working hard in many odd jobs still feels he is not earning enough to feed a family of four. He feels lonely and helpless, with nowhere to turn for guidance.

Similar true stories are plentiful in society. Many of us, sometimes in life, experience this loneliness, hopelessness, and disconnection. However, if we can reconnect to our inner power and the divine power of Nature, we will be empowered again with hope, faith, and guiding light.

Find an opportunity to be alone with nature, e.g., by the beach at night looking up into the star-filled sky, or during a quiet walk early in the morning in an empty park. Do you have a sense of belonging to something much larger, more divine, so much more meaningful than just getting up daily, going to work, going home, having dinner, watching TV, and paying bills?

Do we ever ask ourselves, "Who are we really? What is our true nature?"

We will be amazed to realize we are more than just a physical body. We have an inner power that can change our life and even change the world!

When we know who we really are, most of our daily problems become insignificant and we realize we inherently possess power to achieve whatever we desire.

Look within, not without

To solve daily life problems, most people look for guidance from external sources. It is understandable. However, if we rely only on external guidance and do not realize the treasure within, we make the serious mistake of Ali Hafed.

Ali Hafed owned a large farm of orchards, grain fields, and gardens. He was a wealthy and happy man. One day, a Buddhist priest visited Ali. After dinner, they sat down by the fire and chatted. The priest happened to mention that a diamond was worth a lot of money. A small diamond of the size of his thumb could buy a county, and if he had a mine of diamonds, he might be able to influence people to help his son to become king.

That night, Ali Hafed stayed awake all night, feeling unhappy. He felt unhappy not because he lost anything, but because he did not own any mine of diamonds. He woke the priest up early in the morning and asked, "Where can I find a mine of diamonds?"

The priest said, "Why? You are already rich!"

"I want to be immensely rich!"

"Then, go and find a river that runs through white sands, between high mountains. You can find diamonds in those white sands."

"Are there such rivers?"

"Yes, a lot of them out there. Some lead to a mine of diamonds."

"I will go," Ali said.

Then, Ali Hafed sold his farm, left his family, and went in search of diamonds. With money from selling his farm, he went all over the place, from the Mountains of the Moon, around Palestine, wandering on into Europe. His journey was long and tiring. At last, he arrived in Spain when all his money was spent. He was hungry and penniless. He stood on the shore of the Bay of Barcelona, feeling terribly hopeless, staring at the incoming tide.

He could not resist the awful temptation. Then, he jumped down into the river and drowned. Poor man!

At home, the new owner of Ali's farm happened to collect a small "rock" on the sands of a creek running through the farm, which he did not know was a diamond. Months later, the priest came back. Seeing the small "rock" on the table, he happily called, "Ali is back—you found diamonds?"

The new owner came out. "No, Ali is not back, and that is not a diamond."

"I know a diamond when I see one. Where did you pick this one up?"

"At the creek."

They hurried out to the creek and scratched the sands. Oh yes, they found more diamonds here and there. It turned out that was the opening of the largest mine of diamonds on earth: the Golconda!

Poor Ali Hafed!

He did not realize he had the largest mine of diamonds right on this farm at home and went looking for it somewhere else.

Each of us has within an immensely valuable treasure: our true nature. Unaware of it, we are like an absent-minded billionaire wandering in busy city streets begging for a few dollars. The billionaire does not remember he has a huge amount of money in the bank.

We are more than our body

When asked, "Who are we?" we tend to reply, we are such and such a name, our age, our social status, our job, etc. These are what we own, not who we really are. We are the one having that name, age, social status, job, etc. But who are we really?

We are not our bodies, not even our mind, which most people perceive as their true Selves.

There is something in us that is divine and higher than our mortal self. This something is powerful, and it enables the brain, the heart, and all organs to function amazingly.

In a silent night, when we hear a distant temple's bell, we say we hear the sound. However, if the temple's bell did not sound, do we hear it? Yes, we do! Thanks to the ability to hear, we know that there is no bell sounding. The mysterious power enabling this "ability to hear" is our true Self.

A metaphor is the light in a room. When we turn on the electric switch, the light shines in the entire room. What gives light? Is it the switch, or the wire, or the tangible fixture called "the light" on the ceiling? Or is it the electricity that we do not see? The electricity in this case is similar to our true Self.

We have two selves: a tangible self which is our body and an intangible one which is our true Self. Our tangible self is like the electric set that consists of the light switch, the wire, and the light bulb. Our true Self is the electricity. Our mind thinks, reasons, analyzes, judges, etc., but our mind is not us. Our true Self is what enables our mind to think, reason, analyze, judge, etc.

We do not see our true Self, but we can feel its existence.

Get totally relaxed, free of all distractions coming from the five senses and the mind. Close our eyes, and direct our attention into our body. Feel the subtle energy from within and realize that we are beyond the outer form which is our body. In this inward journey, take ourselves deeply into the realm of great stillness, total peace, great power, and vibrant life. Do not start thinking. Feel it. Feel some subtle energy that is formless, limitless, and unfathomable, yet indestructible.

Who We Really Are?

Our true Self and the Universal Self have the same nature

That is our true Self, our real nature.

Feel our connection with the Universal Self

From feeling what our true Self is, we can perceive what all true Selves in the universe are--and thus we reach the immensity of the Universal Self, called God, Buddha, Allah, . . . That is the "entity" we refer to, outside and beyond the box we call religion.

The Universal Self is the source that creates everything in the universe and to which everything comes back when its physical existence ceases. This Universal Self is what enables natural laws to function.

The law of attraction enables the moon to move around the Earth for billions of years. The Universal Self is the power behind the law of attraction. The four seasons of a year keep going through the same cycle every year. The Universal Self is the power behind this phenomenon. What makes the seed of a plant grow to the same plant and produce the same fruit? The Universal Self!

Because the true Self of each living being originates from the Universal Self, we are all connected. In addition, each of us has within an immense potential of creativity, and unlimited organizing power.

More than two thousand years ago, great spiritual leaders—the Buddha, Jesus Christ,

Mohammed, Lao-Tzu, etc.—realized and confirmed this truth.

Some people in recent times also realized the power of the Universal Self.

Ralph Waldo Emerson

Born in 1803, Ralph Waldo Emerson became a Christian minister in 1829. The death of his beloved wife from tuberculosis, only eighteen months after marriage, changed his beliefs. He resigned from the pastorage. Unemployed, with no fallback plan, and in intense sorrow of lost love, he set sail for Europe.

During daytime on the ship, he walked the deck and gazed out at the vast sea, meditating on such questions as "Where can one find peace in time of uncertainty? Who can one turn to for guidance?" At night, he wrote down his insights. He then perceived his real nature is made of the same "core stuff" of whatever-it-is of the universe. This core stuff, he perceived, is the very ground of existence of everything—matter, energy, and consciousness. He felt the "open secret of the universe" and found inner peace and real joy of life. He became an enlightened spiritual writer and lecturer.

To Emerson, the more we study nature, the better we know ourselves. His spiritual teachings have enlightened millions of people for 170 years.

True Wealth

Eckhart Tolle

Until the age of thirty, Eckhart Tolle had lived in continuous anxiety with periodical suicidal depression. He recalled one night; he suddenly felt an intense delineation with the external world. Everything—the vague outlines of the furniture in the dark room, the distant noise of a passing train, seemed so hostile. Everything appeared so disgusting, especially his own existence.

He keenly felt a temptation to commit suicide. He kept repeating to himself, "I cannot live with myself any longer." Then followed a silent period. Suddenly he became aware of a revelation: "Am I one or two? There must be two of me: the 'I' and the 'physical self' that I cannot live with."

And this is important: only one of them is real!

He kept thinking about the "I" that watches the activities of his physical self, i.e., his bodily shell. Although it is invisible, he realized it is his true Self. It is immense and powerful! He found his real identity!

Thereafter, for a while he was left with nothing on this physical world, no relationships, no job, no home, no socially defined identity. However, during the time he spent almost two years on park benches, he was in a state of intense joy solely because he realized he found something most valuable.

Then, he became an international spiritual teacher who has positively changed the lives of millions of people. His teachings and his book *"The Power of Now"* enable millions of people realize their true Selves and the resultant true happiness.

The Universal Self is the divine source of all possibilities, organizing and creating everything in the world. Because we are partakers of the Source of unlimited power, we possess the same unlimited potential power within us. If we can leverage this unlimited power within to do something, we can achieve any goal, even perform wonders. Can we effectively use this potential?

Yes! Below are ways to use the supreme power of the Universal Self.

Use the power of the Universal Self

We can use the power of the Universal Self in three ways. ((a) Have total belief: clear our mind for easy access to potential power, be in tune with our true nature, and have total confidence that the amazing inner power can help us achieve anything,(b) go the extra step in any endeavor for excellence, and (c) most importantly, leverage natural laws.

Clear our mind for easy access to inner power

Remove all negative emotions such as hatred, anger, greed, jealousy, etc. Eradicate all negative thinking such as preconceived opinions, prejudices, worries, doubts, suspicions, etc. Avoid all behaviors and actions deemed harmful or destructive to others.

The logic is that we all are from the same Divine Source (God, Buddha, Allah, Omnipotence, etc.). We are connected to each other. To do harm to others is to harm ourselves. In addition, all negative emotions, negative thinking, destructive behaviors, etc. are hindrances to inner power. Experience it. While worried, nervous, angry, etc., we cannot think clearly because we cannot access the inner power.

In silence, we think better. When we are calm, we feel connected. When we are emotionally aroused, we make bad decisions. The wisdom of our true Self is like a treasure at the bottom of a lake. If the water is tranquil, it is transparent, we can see the treasure. If the water is muddy, or frequently moved by strong winds, we cannot see it.

When the sky is cloudy, gloomy, we cannot see sunlight. When the sky is clear, everything on the ground enjoys nourishing sunlight. Before doing anything (think, speak, act), be silent, clear our mind for easy tuning to the Source of wisdom within. This may take several seconds (10, 20, or longer).

Cook, the CEO of Apple, has practiced it for years. A *Fortune* article in 2018 said that in meetings, Cook often pauses for long, uncomfortable periods, when all you hear is the sound of his tearing the wrapper of the energy bars he constantly eats.

Bezos, the founder, and CEO of Amazon, has also used this awkward silence, but in a less uncomfortable way. It reflects in waiting time at the beginning of meetings, reportedly up to 30 minutes, while he reads printed memos in silence. The idea is to allow participants time to peruse the memo, to think, and even to scribble notes of initial thoughts and ideas—all without interruption.

Elon Musk, the CEO of Tesla Motors, often takes up to even 15 seconds to think before giving an answer when he is interviewed.

Steve Jobs, the co-founder of Apple Inc., once took almost 20 seconds to respond to a personal attack.

The value is that all these men deliver a perfect response.

We live in a world that demands instant gratification. Emails should be answered on the same day. Zoom meetings must be attended at an exact time, bills must be paid now or incur stiff penalties, etc. All of these time-demanding pressures block our access to true inner power required for whatever we do.

Practice clearing your mind for good decisions.

Be in tune with our true nature

Each of us and everything around us is created by the same Divine Source. The individual Self of each is a partaker of this Divine Source. Observe this individual Self in everything around us. Stop and silently feel that divinity in a flower blooming in our garden, lovingly look at the eyes of our dog—we can feel its divine soul that we feel within us. Form the habit of communicating with the Divine Source in everything we happen to meet.

Whenever possible, and on a daily basis, go into a quiet place. In the silence, we are undisturbed by any agitations of physical senses and are in a receptive attitude. Calmly, quietly, and expectantly tune into the immensity of the Divine Source. Feel it taking possession of our soul, then our mind, and slowly manifesting in every part of our body. Feel that quiet, peaceful, illuminating power to harmonize our body, mind, and soul with the world. Maintain this harmony in all our daily activities: working, walking, talking, resting, sleeping, etc. That way, the power of Divine Source is with us at all times.

Have total confidence that the amazing inner potential can help us achieve anything

Have faith that with inner power we can do anything. Faith is the awareness that we have amazing power enabling us to do anything. Experience it. Without this faith, most tasks appear difficult or impossible. With this faith, most tasks appear doable, apparently impossible tasks become possible. Faith! It is the faith implied in the statement, "If you have faith, even as small as a mustard seed, you can move mountains." Such a faith means miracles to us.

Have total confidence that the amazing potential within us will help us do anything. A person hit by a stroke who becomes paralyzed can recover normal activities in a shorter time than otherwise if he has faith in his inner power. The belief of two boxers of equal fighting skills on the ring determines the result of the match. The man who wins is the one who believes he will win.

Take the extra step

The second way to use the power of the Universal Self is to take the extra step.

In whatever we are doing, take an <u>extra step</u>. It is the "place" where we use up our normal power and begin to touch the inner power.

When our body and our mind are ready to stop for the day, we say, "No, go extra mile, spend extra minute, exercise extra energy for the extra result." Strive to reach the seemingly unreachable point. This habit makes the difference between the good and the best and identifies the best of the bests.

The seemingly unreachable step is the highest level of one's normal activity that appears beyond our ability. It is the step where connection to inner power is possible!

World-famous cyclist Lance Armstrong won his first victory of Tour de France by exercising this extra step. Never having been a renowned rider, Armstrong was ignored by other mountain-riding contestants. After five and a half miles ascending mountains, all riders were suffering. During the third mountain ascent, Lance was alone, fighting to catch the two top riders in the world.

In the last five miles, Lance had expended almost all the strength in him, still thirty-two seconds behind the two established world-class riders. Exhausted, legs and arms burning with fatigue, struggling to breathe, he told himself, "It's not about the bike. It is my journey back to life!" This empowering thought triggered his inner power. Lance stood up, painfully surged ahead, and gaining momentum, he slowly but surely passed the two leaders. They too tried but could not beat his passing. Lance kept pounding the pedals. He used the extra effort beyond the normal physical limit, and eventually crossed the finish line first. He won. The extra effort is rewarding!

Without this empowering thought, the two leaders slowly fell behind him.

The second aspect is emotion—a positive emotion, e. g., love, faith, altruism, heroism, etc. If we reach the deeply felt emotion at its highest level, the extra emotional step, we will be empowered with the inner power.

During World War Two, prime minister Winston Churchill addressed Parliament about how to protect England against the inherent invasion of the powerful German army. After an ardent elaboration, he paused several seconds, then said with deep conviction: "We shall fight on the streets, we shall fight on the seas, we shall protect our island! We shall not surrender!" All stood up and applauded explosively.

Everyone was deeply touched because he himself was deeply motivated by the good cause: "Defend our beloved country at any cost against the invading force." People were touched, truly aroused because what he said resonated with the inner value within each.

He got this convincing power because he reached the normally unreachable point of his emotion, totally immerged in the conviction to fight to death for his country.

The artist who reaches his deepest inner being will

touch the hearts of listeners, viewers, or readers. We have listened to the average and good singer and feel good. However, the singer who has reached this seemingly unreachable feeling, totally immerged into the true feeling of the song, really melts our hearts!

Only when an orator truly believes in what he is saying, devoting his entire soul and life, fully passionate in his speaking will be able to sink the valuable message into the audience's mind, to lift them up from their seats to ardently applaud him!

If we want to touch people's hearts with an emotion, we must reach this deeply felt emotion first. We must truly convince ourselves first. We must reach the seemingly unreachable but must-reach point of a positive emotion!

Leveraging natural laws

The third way to use the power of the Universal Self is by leveraging natural laws, which are cause-and-effect relationships. Because something happens, the effect is "something will happen." Everything around us is strictly operated by natural laws. Pay attention, and you will discover them. As long as there is a relationship between a cause and an effect, we have a natural law.

A natural law is absolute. It always works, regardless of whether we want it or not, or are aware of it or not! A natural law is universal. It works anywhere in the world. It works at all times. A natural law does not budge. It is not subject to debate!

The law "If we spend more than our income, we will have financial difficulties" is true for anyone in any country, and for any generation. It always works.

An employee who always cares for the interests of the company and its customers will guarantee his job. He will have a better chance for a raise, promotion, and a bright career. A business owner who truly cares about the satisfaction of his customers instead of just the money will be fairly rewarded in the long run.

Leveraging natural laws empowers us to achieve desired effects. Leveraging means we create "the cause" to enjoy "its effect." Our feelings confirm whether we successfully leverage or not: we feel good and confident that we will get the expected results.

Briefly, to use our inner power, we must:

- clear our mind for easy access,

- be in tune with our true nature,

- have total confidence that the amazing potential within us will help us achieve anything,

- go extra step in any endeavor for excellence, and

- leverage natural laws.

In summary, realize we all have an amazing inner power and can leverage this power to become a truly wealthy person.

3

Setting and Achieving Goals

This chapter is about setting a goal and achieving it. There will be no more worries, anxieties, doubts, fears, etc., about achieving a specific goal. We will discuss the importance of having a clear and specific goal and a natural law empowering us to achieve it.

A group of 1953 graduates of Yale University were asked if they had a clear, specific written down goal with a plan for achieving it. Only 3% said "Yes." Twenty years later, another survey of the same graduates showed that the wealth of this small group of 3% was greater than the total wealth of the remaining 97% combined.

What is the message?

Common sense helps answering. We go nowhere if we just get into a car not knowing where we want to go. Similarly, consider two ships sailing out of port. One ship, having a definite destination, will get there with a chance of 99.9%. The other ship sails out of the port, leaving the engine on and aimlessly going around, it will certainly get nowhere.

In 1908, Napoleon Hill was asked by Andrew Carnegie, one of the world's richest men, to go interview the world's wealthiest people to find out the single secret that they used for their success. Twenty years later, he revealed one requirement of this secret: "Having a specific goal and a definite plan for achieving it."

What is the power behind this "secret"?

The power is our subconscious. Our mind has two levels: the explicit conscious and the hidden subconscious. We are aware of the activities of the conscious mind—for example, when we think, we know we are thinking. But we are unaware of the activities of the subconscious—for example, when we dream, we do not know we are dreaming. However, the subconscious shapes our life's destiny, and we can influence our subconscious with a valuable tool: our thinking.

Compared to the conscious mind, the subconscious is very powerful, like the whole wonderful underwater world compared to the thin surface of the ocean.

The subconscious classifies and records everything that ever happened in our life since our birth, including feelings and thoughts. The information will be retrieved and used when needed. Note that these recorded information influence our feelings and actions, hence our destiny. Our subconscious strongly affects our thinking, feelings, and actions. For example, on the bus a young man happens to see a pretty girl wearing a light green dress. He likes her, thinking she is cute. Later in his life, he has completely forgotten the incident, but somehow he loves the same light green color without knowing why. His pleasant feeling was recorded by his subconscious.

When seeded in our subconscious, a thought will grow like a plant in a garden plot. The subconscious is like a fertile plot of land. Whatever planted there will be more sure-footed with repetition and will develop abundantly. Notice that whether a thought is constructive or destructive is immaterial. Constructive as well as destructive thought will grow and develop without discrimination. Hence, as experts say, the pessimists are right, and the optimists are equally right. Whatever we think, we become and are. Hence, **when a goal is planted in our mind and constantly reviewed, the subconscious will help this goal materialize.**

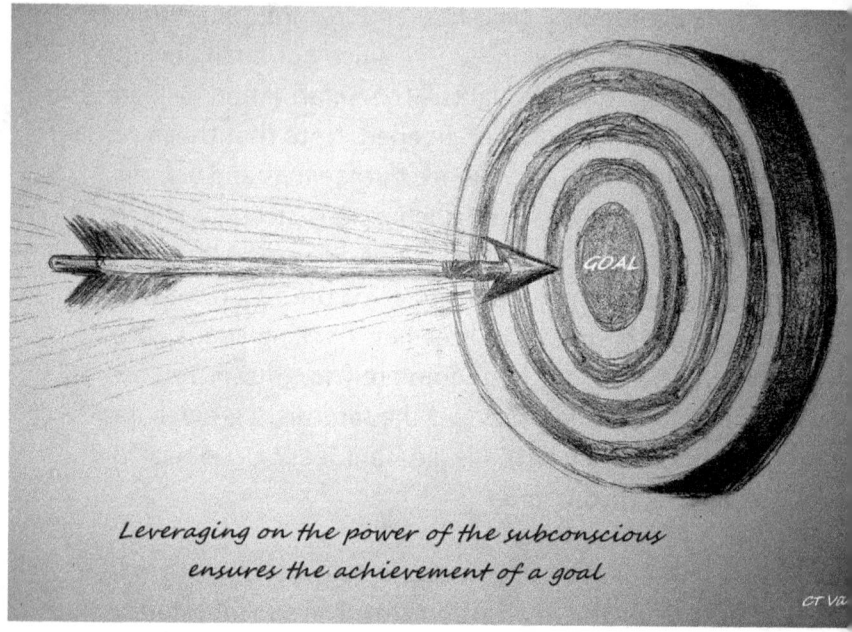

Leveraging on the power of the subconscious ensures the achievement of a goal

Incorporating more characteristics of the subconscious, the following steps ensure the achievement of a goal.

Four practical steps for achieving a goal:

1. Have a goal specifically stated in detail.

The goal must be specific. This is similar to the functioning of a computer. A computer is an able servant. It can do many tasks with one requirement: the order to fulfill must be specific. If the order is ambiguous, it just sits there, doing nothing. The slightest confusion in the order renders the computer useless. Our subconscious is like the power behind the computer. It works the same way and is more powerful. If we desire to accumulate an amount of money, the specific goal should be, e.g., $50,000, by December 15, 20xx. If we wants to master an occupation, the specific goal should be, e.g., becoming an electronic engineer, able to easily perform all related tasks by May 31, 20xx. As soon as the goal is specifically stated, the inherent organizing ability within us starts working, offers an initial plan, and attracts information to achieve that goal.

2. *State what we will do to achieve the desired goal.*

Plan what we will do. In addition, our goal must be socially beneficial. If our goal benefits the community, we have a good chance of achieving it. Any goal harmful or destructive to the community has the seed of failure. This is harmonious with the natural law of giving and receiving. We cannot get something for nothing. We must give something. In addition, we all are connected; if our goal is beneficial to society, it benefits ourselves. If the goal is the accumulation of $50,000, what we will do is, e.g., cleaning houses for clients in the community. In this case, we stimulate our inner power to figure out how to get clients, how many hours we must work daily, and adjust our intended service accordingly.

3. *Foster the intensity of desire and carry out any doable actions.*

Intense emotions connect us to our subconscious. If a goal is specifically stated and backed up with a burning desire, firm expectation, and total belief, we will more easily connect to the subconscious. When we strive to clearly visualize getting and living the expected results, the law of attraction will gain momentum and attract more ideas and opportunities from the vast subconscious for us to improve the existing plan.

Upon receiving ideas about doable tasks for the goal, perform them as soon as possible. The main reason why many people fail is lack of action. They just think about the goal without doing anything. The subconscious works to deliver useful ideas and a definite plan, but we must transform them to reality with action. Everything is created twice; the first creation in our mind and the second in reality.

Feeling good about a doable task is a valuable hint that of the subconscious is pointing us in the right direction.

4. *Repeat the above 3 steps until the goal is achieved.*

We might not achieve our goal in a short time. No problem; repeat the first 3 steps. Gather more information, clarify what still confuses us, and think further. With each repetition, there will be improvements. Incorporate new improvements after each repetition and we will move closer and closer to achieving the goal. Keep repeating the above 3 steps until we feel total faith that we WILL achieve the goal.

Three empowering concepts

The above four steps will be empowered if we incorporate the following three concepts:

The evolutionary process

Evolution means small improvements, adapting smoothly with unexpected changes. This is analogous to going from point A, where we are now, to point B, the intended destination. If there are no unexpected incidents, we go from A to B smoothly. However, in reality, there are so many unknown and unexpected variables. We must adapt, we must adjust our planned activities to new developments. Hence, our path from A to B might be different than planned. In addition, goal B very likely is modified to be a better one, say B1, B2, etc. The outcome is that we will achieve our intended goal, or a better one. But, sooner or later, we will achieve our goal.

Any unexpected development in the process may show a natural and easy path. To reach a goal faster, we should follow this path.

Ten years after being established, Marriott Corporation had nine successful restaurants. Its goal was to double the number of restaurants in three years. The goal was promising, with well-trained employees and management. However, something happened at the 8th restaurant close to the Hoover Airport in Washington, DC. At the beginning, a few passengers stopped by and ordered food for their flights. The number of such passengers grew.

In a trip to check on the restaurant, the founder of Marriott Corporation, Mr. Willard Marriott was aware of the development and wanted to pursue further. The next day he went to the Eastern Air Transport and arranged for the 8th restaurant to regularly deliver packaged food to the airport. He succeeded.

The business grew unexpectedly. In a few months, the food-delivery business developed to American Airlines with more than twenty-two daily flights. Marriott continued to grow the business to more than 200 airports.

Marriott leveraged the natural path of the evolutionary process to achieve unexpected results, which is hundreds of times better than the intended goal of doubling the number of Marriott restaurants!

During this evolutionary process for achieving a goal, we naturally mingle with the flow of new developments. Often we achieve a goal faster, or even a better goal than intended if we follow the easy and natural path.

In the above four-step process, the improving mechanism is embedded. It is human nature to keep doing better and better at whatever we are doing.

Crossing the consciousness threshold

Some might ask, "When do we have total faith we will achieve the goal?" There is a consciousness level referred to as the consciousness threshold, the crossing of which is critical.

We can identify the threshold by checking our feelings to reveal where we are relative to the threshold. Below this threshold are fear, worry, doubt, anxiety, and uncertainty. Above the threshold are comfort, poise, belief, and faith. If we have already crossed the threshold, we have convinced ourselves that we can and will achieve our goal.

In the process, the subconscious has gathered all needed information and creatively organized them into a plausible plan. We feel its logic, its certainty, and know we will attain our goal.

If we indeed have crossed the consciousness threshold, we FEEL and KNOW we will get what we intend, and we do not hope or wish that we will get it.

Crossing the consciousness threshold for wealth, we become wealth conscious. A wealth-conscious person knows he will be wealthy even when he scratches for money to pay bills. The mentality of a wealth-conscious person must be "knowing," and not "hoping" or "wishing."

This is similar to a success-conscious person. When a gifted singer walks out to the stage to sing, she knows she will capture the heart of the audience before she starts the first musical note. When an eloquent orator steps to the microphone to give a speech, he knows he will touch the spirit of the audience before he speaks the first word! The gifted singer and the eloquent orator are success conscious people.

To a success conscious person, success is guaranteed. To a wealth conscious person, wealth is guaranteed. Achieving our goal is guaranteed when we have crossed the consciousness threshold.

Resolving a dilemma: the law of vibration and the "non-having" thought

Some will say, "I have always thought about being wealthy for many years, why do I still struggle with not having enough money? It contradicts the belief 'what we think we are'".

How can this dilemma be resolved?

It can be resolved by the law of vibration. What is the

law of vibration? Each thought has a vibrating frequency, and thoughts of the same vibrating frequencies will be attracted to each other. If we constantly think and feel good about being wealthy, we will attract all information needed for being wealthy. The above dilemma is created by our thinking of "struggle with not having enough money" and feel bad about it. Remember, we get what we think about and especially feel it! We want more money, but by thinking about not having enough money, we contradict ourselves, being pulled in opposite directions. It is like we want classical music but tune our radio to the station playing rock music. Of course, we cannot hear classical music. Thinking about "struggling with not having enough money" and feeling bad about it will not get us more money.

The message is to think purely about what we want, without the slightest thought about what we do not want. We cannot say, "I want to be a manager of my department" while simultaneously thinking "but maybe the boss doesn't like me." It defeats the purpose! We cannot say "I want to become an expert in my field of specialization" while simultaneously thinking "I might be able to do that, if I am not too old to improve my knowledge and learn new skills." This thinking diminishes the power of thought.

Real-life examples

A man is admired by all his coworkers. He has thorough

knowledge of his company, its products, markets, and competitors. He has spent time understanding the company's customers and their problems. In addition, he has a good manner and a good personality. Obviously, he is an outstanding employee.

When asked how he was motivated to acquire all these qualifications, he replied that upon being hired by this company a few years back, he decided to shoot for the position of a district manager. He has been doing everything he can to be the man qualified for this job. He constantly thinks about his goal and he does anything deemed necessary to get closer to the goal.

In 1922, Jennings Randolph, a graduate of Salem College, was deeply inspired by a message from Dr. Napoleon Hill of "having a specific goal and a clear plan for achieving it." He was sitting in the audience of graduates listening to Dr. Hill's commencement address. He figured out there and then exactly the position he wanted to have in life.

Later, he admitted that the message profoundly inspired him to become who he wanted to become: a congressman. Then, he became an important factor in Franklin D. Roosevelt's administration. Thirty-five years later, the same message helped him become an executive of a leading airline of the nation, then a United States senator from West Virginia. Successive positions were likely his ascending goals.

In summary, achieving a goal might be difficult, but it is guaranteed if we leverage the power of our subconscious, the evolutionary process, the law of vibration, and the law of action. In addition, beware of the consciousness threshold we must cross in the process.

So far, we have discussed the foundation: the source of money, the inner power we possess, and the guaranteed way to achieve a goal. The remaining chapters will discuss ways to empower our earning ability.

4
Using Natural Talents

This chapter offers a way to turn our work into pleasure, a vocation into a vacation. Yet, job performance can be even greater.

Although we all have the same inner potential, each of us is unique. Nobody in the world has the same DNA or fingerprint as anyone else. Similarly, each person has a set of unique natural talents defined as the ability to do something effectively, enjoyably, and easily. We have acquired natural talents since birth. We can perform well certain tasks without learning, like ducks can naturally swim in the water.

Using Natural Talents

*Each person was born
with some natural talents*

A young man enjoys telling fairy tale stories (which he heard from his uncle) to children. Wherever he goes, he can easily gather a group of children to sit around him listening with fascination to his stories. He admits he can just tell the stories and naturally attract children. He himself enjoys doing it very much. Storytelling, to him, is like a duck naturally swimming in the water! "Using body language, emotions, and speaking tone to relate a story as if it is actually happening" is this young man's natural talent.

If we can discover our natural talents and use them in our job, we enjoy every workday of the week. We do not have to wait until Friday to expect a fun weekend, because any job task performed with natural talents brings deep pleasure. Activities at our job are like the fun activities of a vacation.

How can we discover our natural talents?

Hints revealing our natural talents are plentiful in our daily lives. Just pay attention. Plain and explicit, they will be recognized.

The first hint is the *ease* of doing something. The talented American baseball player Babe Ruth, at fifteen years old, felt irritated when watching a player performing badly, from his perception. Coach Matthias said, "Ruth, if you think you can do better, go out and try!" Never playing baseball before, Babe appeared hesitant but confidently went out to try anyway. He did great. Later, Babe confessed, "At that moment, I KNOW the task is naturally easy." That was the hint of Babe Ruth's natural talent: "the ability to coordinate the movements of limbs and body to perform an intended task."

If we feel naturally easy when doing something, we have a natural talent for doing it.

The second hint is the intense *enjoyment* we feel

when doing something. An engineer in Castro Valley, California works for a big corporation. His most exciting activity after work is the opportunity to diagnose and fix the problems of used cars that he occasionally bought. He spends almost all his spare time at this hobby. His joy peaks when he finds out the reason why the car stopped working and a way to fix it. "Finding the root cause of a problem and resolving it" is his natural talent.

When we do something that we lose ourselves in, not keeping track of time, never feeling tired until we receive physical warning signals from the body, then the ability to do what we are doing is our natural talent. We normally get a lot done on the weekend, because we are free to exercise our natural talents.

The third hint is our *effectiveness* when doing something. We just do it, without trying or struggling and it turns out to be highly effective. As mentioned, like a duck in the water, it just swims and does not try to swim. When a natural talented singer sings, her singing touches the heart of listeners even she has not attended any training class in singing yet.

The English comic actor Charlie Chaplin was a natural performer. At five, he was pushed to the stage to replace his mother when her voice suddenly cracked and could not continue. Born a natural performer, he acted and sang two songs, unexpectedly amusing and surprising a tough audience of soldiers. Charlie had to pause in between singing to pick up coins thrown onto the stage for him. His career took off after that night. Charlie Chaplin's natural talent is "using his gesture and body language to effectively amuse people."

Here is a suggestion. Try a lot of activities. If what we do seems so naturally easy, enjoying, or effective, stop and think, "The ability to do what I am doing could be my natural talent!" Then, dig further into our past activities to confirm our natural talents.

Categorizing natural talents

Each natural talent can be classified as of one of five categories of our daily activities: working theme, communicating with people, relating to people, functioning, and leading people.

In each category, we have a natural way to get an intended result.

Working theme

We use a working theme (i.e., how we think, feel, or act) to begin an activity. A working theme may be intuitive. Tom Rath calls the combining set of "thinking, feeling, and behaving" a theme. He lists 34 talent themes. For example, if our theme is "achiever," we begin with the question of what to achieve. We feel a constant need for achievement. We must achieve something by the end of the day in order to feel good about ourselves. A day with no achievement makes us feel like a loser. Another theme is "intellection." If we are an intellection-based person, we begin a task by thinking, we like to think. We enjoy time alone and constantly contemplating a problem until we find a satisfactory answer. This is our task-starting mentality or talent theme.

We recommend reading his book *"Strengths Finder 2.0"* for a complete description of all 34 talent themes.

Our working theme is the first category of our natural talents.

Communication

How do we convey a message to others? We can use words, pictures, sounds, or body language and gestures. For each, there are different means, e.g., with words, we can write, converse, teach, broadcast, etc. With pictures, we can draw, paint, design, carve, etc. With sounds, we can compose, sing, play an instrument, etc. With body language and gestures, we can act, play sports, etc.

Of these ways to communicate, there is a set of abilities that is natural to us, and which meets the definition of "natural" in three aspects: ease, enjoyment, and efficiency. This subset of "how to communicate" is our natural talents in communication.

Relating to people

How do we establish rapport with others? We can do it better with a group of people, even stranger(s) at the first meeting, or we can do it more effectively one-on-one with a person, or we can establish rapport better with someone we have met several times.

The way we relate to others that makes us feel naturally easy, enjoyable, and effective, is our natural talent.

Ways of functioning

What are the ways we use time and space to get an intended result?

How do we organize time and space? Are we good in creating, imagining, inventing, developing, planning, managing? Are we good at hand-arm coordination, operating coordination, hand-finger coordination? In addition, we might function differently such as tutoring, serving others, counseling, evaluating people, projecting the future, negotiating, selling, promoting, researching, working with numbers, reasoning, analyzing, evaluating, synthesizing, making decisions, etc.

Among all these ways to function, there are some that

we can perform naturally with ease, joy, and effectiveness. They are our natural talents to function.

Leading people

There are two kinds of leaders: the supervisor and the influencer. The leader as supervisor directs and oversees the activities and behaviors of others. The leader as influencer influences the activities and behaviors of others by demonstrating excellence, inspiring by setting examples.

We can naturally lead as supervisor, or as influencer, or both. The style with which we feel easiest, most enjoyable, and most effective is our natural talent in leading others. Note that leadership can apply to any role, position, or title.

Above are five categories of performing a task at work or in daily activities.

How to apply natural talents to our job

If we can use natural talents in our occupation, a job is no longer a struggling battle to earn a living. Every workday is Friday now! How?

John Brady and Jay Carty, two experts in the field, recommend the rule of 60/40. It means sixty percent of our activities should be performed with our natural talents. This is possible because we inherently have natural talents in each of the five aspects of any activity we perform. Just discover (as instructed previously) and use them.

Use natural talents to perform 60% tasks of our job and team up with people having natural talents to perform the remaining 40%.

After we discover our natural talents, apply them in the appropriate aspects of our job (theme, communication, relation, function, or leadership) and observe the feedback. Does it result in enjoyment, ease, and effectiveness? If it does, keep using and developing these talents at work. If it does not, repeat the discovery process.

Keep doing this until our work becomes enjoyable, like a vacation.

In summary, we all have unique natural talents. Discover and use them to enjoy our work and brighten our lives.

5
Becoming an Expert

Top expertise

A blackout happened in a small city of the USA South, lasting many days in a row. Electrical engineers of the company tried various solutions, but the lights still did not come back. A retired engineer was called upon to help. He came over, walked around, and observed the power plant a few times. Finally, he stopped, and with a small hammer he knocked three times on a pipe.

To everyone's relief, the lights came back! He later billed the management $300,003, itemized as $3 for three knocks, and $300,000 for knowing where to knock.

"Knowing where to knock" is the top expertise we must achieve in our field of specialization.

How to achieve top expertise

People in the same profession are worth differently. Among all custodians, there are not-so-good ones doing a lousy job and good ones doing an excellent job. Among all restaurant owners, some have a long waiting line of customers, and others have empty tables most of the time. Among all lawyers, some have a long list of appointments, yet some struggle to occasionally get a few customers. This difference exists in any profession.

The difference is the level of expertise of people in the same profession. How do we move up on the ladder of expertise? The compound effect makes the difference.

The compound effect

After years in the same company, employees have achieved different levels of expertise. Some, with years of seniority, have job knowledge and skills of the first year multiplied many times over! Some, with just a few years in the job, can perform almost any tasks required by the company. The former keep doing for years the same thing they learned the first year; the latter has continuously learned on the job. Even a little bit every day, the learning adds up, compounding with time. That is the power of compound effect.

A sweeping forest wildfire starts with a tiny flame, quickly spreads, and compounds. The fire gains momentum and turns wild. The same compound effect creates destructive hurricanes and floods.

A hypothetical story shows that power. Suppose we are hired by a company for 30 months with two options of getting paid. Option one is $100,000 a month. Option two is $0.01 the first month and the payment of the following month is twice of the payment of the previous month. In other words, the second month $0.02, the third month $0.04, the fourth month $0.08, etc. Which option should we choose? If we choose option one, the total payment from 30 months of employment is $3,000,000. However, this is a bad choice because the total payment of option two is far greater. Using a financial formula or by multiplying $0.01 of the first payment by 2 for 30 times, we get the-30th-month's payment as $10,737,418.24. That is only the payment of the 30th month! It is more than 3.5 times the total payment of option one!

That is the result of the power of compound effect. Simply put, anything growing at certain growth rate per period will compound the effect of growing. If it grows consistently with time, the effect in the last period is astounding. "Compound" means the growth of a period is based on the accumulated result of the previous period. In the above story, we use compound interest formula, where $0.01 grows at the rate of 100% a month for 30 months.

However, the growth rate of 100% is unrealistic.

For practical and realistic application of the power of compound effect, assume we can learn and grow our specialized knowledge and skills by 1 percent a day. Note that "specialized knowledge" refers to the knowledge or skills needed to succeed in a special field.

One percent daily increase in specialized knowledge is reasonable; we can easily do it by reading materials, watching and learning from better people at work. We can also correct today's performance to do better the following day.

The job performance of today is better than yesterday, and tomorrow is better than today, etc. What happens after a year? Using the compound interest formula in Finance, the result shows we become thirty-seven times more knowledgeable and skillful than the first day! In no time, we definitely become a top expert in our occupation.

To be more realistic, suppose we can learn and improve our knowledge and skills by 10 percent a month. Using the financial computation in the form of the well-known rule, "the rule of 72 in finance", our expertise will double every seven-month period. The rule is as follows: if something grows at a rate of 10 percent a month then the number of months for this "something" to double is equal to 72 divided by 10, i.e., 7.2 months.

The logic is "New learning helps us understand more

about our job and occupation. Any additional learning facilitates further learning. As time passes, our knowledge and skills compound and grow exponentially." The power of the compound effect is amazing!

With time, compound effect will multiply a seed into a forest

Our goal is achieving top expertise in our occupation. Top expertise, once acquired, is referred to as the "cookie cutter" in a profession. Thereafter, we can keep using it massively to obtain massive results. That is "the fruit" of compound effect.

Here is a practical way to apply the compound effect to obtain the "cookie cutter": we learn from solving any need or any problem arising from doing our job. Facing a problem, we think of a way to resolve it. Do not let the problem stay on our way. Be determined to resolve it. When the problem is fresh, and related information for a solution is readily available, very likely we can solve it. The solution will not only facilitate many aspects of our future work performance, but we also learn something new. Then another problem comes up, and we resolve it. One by one, another after another is resolved; each will help us move up higher and higher to excellence.

Fixing our eyes on the level of expertise in our profession, we can identify problems on the path there, and solve them one at a time. That is how time propels us to expertise at an accelerating pace.

Learn something new and helpful to our career, even a small helpful hint. Keep learning consistently. Good results will come beyond our expectation. Make time our best partner!

Learn not only the knowledge directly required by our job but also any related information that helps us to perform our job better. For example, a janitor must learn how to use cleaning materials most effectively, how to maintain a facility clean at all times, and how to keep himself from being infected by all messes left by careless users. An attorney must learn all laws pertinent to his legal field and how to find out the truth from piles of contradicting and confusing facts, and how to indirectly get to the truth from whatever witnesses tell or do not want to tell him.

The intent is to resolve all confusions or problems which arise in doing our job until there is none, not even the slightest confusion, in our understanding. Then, all are systematically and totally resolved. We have obtained the "cookie cutter"!

Success stories with compound effect

Miss Tania of Dallas

After graduating with a Bachelor of Arts, Miss Tania came to work at the headquarter of a chain of pizza restaurants in Dallas, Texas. One of her job tasks was to scrutinize the financial statements for the financial health of each restaurant. She developed a thourough understanding of the task and kept learning more every day. Finally, she easily discovered the source of financial problems as well as the financial strengths of each restaurant.

In addition, she figured out strategy to turn a troubled restaurant to a profitable one. She contributed significantly to the profits of the company and hence got a grant to study for a Master of Business Administration degree at Harvard University. Here she learned how to hire competent managers.

Then, she came back to work for the company for a few more years. Later, she bought a few troubled restaurants from the company for herself, turned them into profitable ones, and hired talented managers to run them. Leveraging the talents of competent managers, she not only freed herself from constant supervision of her restaurants, but also accumulated some capital and had time to hunt for more restaurants that she could buy. She kept on learning and using her success formula to grow her business.

In about ten years, she has built a system of successful pizza restaurants and become a multi-millionaire businesswoman. Successes compound to more and greater successes.

Sam Walton of Walmart

Another example is Sam Walton, the founder of the worldwide chain of retail stores of variety merchandise, Walmart. When he opened the first store in Bentonville, Arkansas, he did not know much about the retail business. However, he focused on learning more and quickly applied his new learning to increase his store's revenue.

First, he read all magazines and books about retail. He admired a retail store named Sterling Store, across the street, managed by John Dunham. Almost daily, he went there to learn and came back to apply valuable ideas into his store. He also went to Kmart, then a big and successful retail store, to learn more. Later, when traveling abroad to Hong Kong, Singapore, Malaysia, and Europe, the favorite places he came to visit first were also retail stores. That was his lifelong pursuit—keep learning and applying to his retail business.

His original store in Bentonville, Arkansas grew into a worldwide chain. He left a legacy after his death.

Consistent improvement with time

Time is critical in building a career for a person who learns something new daily. We waste time, a valuable asset, if we are doing the same thing over and over, with no improvement at all.

It is critical that we are consistently improving over time, skipping no period in the process. In the 30-day-employment story, if we skip a single month, i.e., the money does not double that month, the 30th payment will be $5,368,709.12. It is reduced by half!

On the path to excellence, we also need to think out of the box, to do something different than what is routinely done. We must think creatively. The next chapter discusses how to come up with creative ideas that revolutionize our profession.

6
Creative Ideas

Objective

We want to continuously be better at doing what we are doing. "Better" at doing something means getting more results with the same or less effort.

In 1701, Jethro Tull invented the seeding machine to plant seeds in many rows simultaneously. In the 1730s, Charles Townshend thought of rotating crops. Cyrus McCormick invented a machine to accelerate harvesting. These inventions helped to get more results with the same or less efforts. They increased agricultural production and led to the Agricultural Revolution lasting more than fifty years.

The invention of machines helped with manufacturing the first automobile in 1886. The invention then led to the Industrial Revolution, which lasted for few hundred years. The Industrial Revolution consists of four phases: using water and steam power, using electric power, leveraging on digital revolution, and advances in artificial intelligence, etc. These inventions furthered massive production.

"Better" also means a completely different way of doing things to achieve more and better results with less effort. The Information Revolution has achieved both with the Internet, World Wide Web, Google, Facebook, YouTube, smart phone, etc., and still going on at an accelerating pace.

These inventions are revolutionizing creative ideas which often begin with responding to pressing needs of humanity, significantly changing the way we are living. Imagine sending a message reaching many recipients within seconds—a giant step from snail mail to email.

Fortunately, each of us has a potential for achieving such creativity.

The law of attraction and multicausal relationships are underlying factors. The law of attraction, previously discussed, states, "like attracts like," meaning, "information, emotion, thought, or action" attracts "same nature information, emotion, thought, or action." If we treat people badly, they tend to treat us badly. If we treat people with loving kindness, they tend to treat us with loving kindness.

What about multicausal relationships? We have discussed causal relationships. It means because something happens, something else will happen as a result. It is a linear relationship. For example, the law of giving and receiving, stating "if we provide a useful service to others, we will be fairly rewarded" is a causal relationship. It shows, "satisfying a need of others" results in "earning a fair reward, often in the form of money." A multicausal relationship is not a simple linear relationship. A creative idea, the result of multicausal relationships, is the collective result of many causes hidden from us.

The following facts explain further.

The travel of ideas through space and time

Ideas travel through space and time. Among a group of monkeys living on an isolated island near Japan, one learned to wash sweet potatoes just dug from the ground before eating. This monkey then taught another, who in turn taught another. Soon, many of them knew how to do it.

When the majority of monkeys on this island were aware of that "discovery," a group of monkeys on another isolated island naturally knew how to do it. This incident reveals that ideas can travel through space.

In addition, ideas also travel through time. Before Thomas Edison's invention of electric light, there were at least twenty people perceiving the creative idea of electric light.

The space around us perceived as "nothing" in fact contains plenty of information and energy, which are "materials" for forming anything in our lives. A specific "item" manifests because its "seed material" attracts materials having the same vibrational frequency. The results could be tangible things like houses, cars, plants, etc. They could be intangible things like solutions to difficult questions, or creative ideas we wish to achieve.

"Materials" travel through space and time and attract or are attracted to form a specific "item." We can listen to music or news from a radio and can watch pictures from a television because the sound signals and the picture's pixels from the space are combined. However, we cannot see these signals and pixels because they are so small that our naked eyes cannot detect them.

The consciousness nature of all things

Everything we see around us is essentially consciousness. Everything perceived as solid, e.g., tables, computers, people, plants, animals, mountains, rivers, etc., appear and disappear as time goes by. The nature of everything is not physical; their real nature is consciousness.

Nothing we see around us lasts forever. It comes from "nothing" and go back to "nothing." Observe a flower. From nothing on a rose bush, a bud appears. The bud grows into a small rose, blooms beautifully to the peak of its beauty, fades, then with time its petals fall one after another. Finally, the flower disappears into "nothing." Human beings are the same. We are born, grow to maturity, age, and die. There is no exception; with time we all come and go. Everything that appears very solid, like a table, a house, or a city building, will be completely gone to nothing, given a long enough time.

How does a creative idea manifest?

At the beginning, we must have an <u>intent</u> to create something. Intent is the beginning of creation. When we want to lift a chair, we begin with the intent to do so, then we stand up, approach the chair, and actually lift it.

To have a creative idea, intent is the beginning. Intent is powerful and serves as the center of attracting necessary ideas coming from remote places in the universe. We begin with imagining what we want to create, then constantly think about it. Having an intent is like planting a seed in the subconscious. Constantly thinking about the intent is like appropriately watering the seed; then the plant gradually appears.

Attention helps by growing what we pay attention to. If we pay attention to and take a good care of a plant, a relationship, or an idea, related thoughts or actions will be attracted and help them manifest.

The <u>intensity</u> of our thought empowers the attraction. Have a burning desire of getting the creative idea you intend to get. Think of all possible and conceivable ways to get that idea, dig further to clarify any detail, research to get more information, etc. All these activities empower our intention to attract helpful ideas from somewhere in the boundless space and from limitless time of the universe. Sometimes, the needed information is from our subconscious.

After that, let <u>the universe take care of all details</u>. If the intention is intensely strong, it will sufficiently attract related information and create something, which we intended to get.

What considered <u>miracles</u> are merely phenomena happening in the higher worlds, which we cannot understand. The concept of "dimension" helps explain better.

Time is a one-dimensional concept: past, present, and future. Space is a three-dimensional concept: width, length, and height. A being living in a lower-dimensional world cannot understand events happening in a higher-dimensional world. Consider an ant living in a two-dimensional world. Suppose it is crawling on an edge of a piece of paper (which is a two-dimensional world). If we fold the paper, taking the ant from one edge to the opposite one, it experiences a "miracle" because it does not understand what we, a living being in the three-dimensional world, did.

People, used to the three-dimensional world, could possibly perceive events in higher-dimensional one, but not too far. Where we are now will be quite a different place ten years before or later, and totally different fifty or a hundred years from now. The differences are from the introduction of the fourth dimension (time) into our three-dimensional world. What if we are taken to a five, six, or higher and higher-dimensional worlds? We would not understand the manifestation of events in these worlds. It would be miraculous to us!

The dimension concept helps us understand why a revolutionary creative idea can be delivered to us as a miracle. The law of attraction, combined with multicausal effect, explains how everything around us including creative idea, is created.

While a causal relationship is a linear relationship between a cause and an effect, a multicausal effect shows a phenomenon or incident as the result of many events from higher-dimensional worlds collectively contributing to its occurrence. Because all contributing factors are hidden in some inconceivable worlds, the resultant incident is perceived as a coincidence—in this case, the needed creative idea.

Here is an example of a multicausal incident.

Ms. Diem and Mr. Hung were across-the-street neighbors in Vietnam when they were sixteen and seventeen years old and cared for each other dearly. But the chaotic civil war forced them to lose contact with each other. They wished hopelessly to reunite but went different ways in life, getting married to different spouses. After the fall of Southern Vietnamese government in 1975, both couples happened to arrive in the US. Ms. Diem lived in Houston, Texas and Mr. Hung in Nashville, Tennessee.

In 2004, Hung's spouse passed away, and after retirement he moved to San Jose, CA. Because of the high cost of living in San Jose, Hung moved to Houston in 2009. In 2011, Diem's spouse passed away. In 2013, Diem called an unknown telephone number in the family notebook, out of curiosity. She was pleasantly surprised to recognize Mr. Hung's voice on the other side of the phone! They found each other again and the feeling strangely stayed the same for both. Two years later, they got married and lived together in their seventies.

Many incidents collectively contributed to and caused their reunion: the death of each spouse and its timing, the reason that Hung decided to move away from Nashville, the cost of living caused him to move from San Jose to Houston, the curiosity leading to the telephone call of Ms. Diem. Had one of these incidents not happened, there would not be the reunion! That is what we call a multicausal effect.

This example is not isolated. Many events occurring in our lives are multicausal results too.

Multicausal results are hints from the Universal Self that the expected creative ideas are hidden somewhere around us.

The relationships between events in the multidimensional world are immediate and unmitigated (i.e., their strength does not diminish with time and distance). Immediate means time is irrelevant, unmitigated means space is irrelevant. Some dogs have such relationships with their owners. They wait at the front door ten minutes to hours before their owners arrive home. That happens even if the owners go home unexpectedly. The dogs immediately and fully sense the owners' intention to go home.

That relationship is also observed in human beings. While talking to Dr. Deepak Chopra, one of his patients suddenly felt a piercing pain in his stomach and fell rolling around the floor. Later, he found out that at exactly the same moment of the incident, his mother had been mugged in Philadelphia and stabbed in the abdomen. He had strong connection with his mother and felt her pain as his own.

Because a multicausal effect is immediate and unmitigated, a creative idea often manifests as a flashing thought.

Practically, how do we facilitate the process of achieving a creative idea?

Having an intent is the beginning. Upon receiving an intense intention, the universe will take over and work on the details, generating related multicausal effects in the multidimensional world leading to the intended creative ideas.

To receive our intended creative ideas, we need to pay attention to accidental incidents or coincidences from the universe. They are valuable hints.

Always aware of what we are looking for (hence, enhancing the power of attraction), we can maximize the number of hints delivered by the multidimensional world.In his book *"The Luck Factor",* Dr. Richard Wiseman advises us to develop a strong network of friends and acquaintances, to have a relaxed attitude toward life, and to open to new experiences in our lives.

Creative Ideas

To accelerate the manifestation of an intended creative idea, we need to facilitate hints from the universe. We need to maximize our contacts with people and happenings around us.

To develop and maintain a strong network of friends and acquaintances, be spontaneous to create opportunities to meet new people. Be open and friendly, we can meet people who know people who know more people. Research shows that a person knows about 200 others by first name. Hence, new contacts help create a large network of friends and acquaintances, which we maintain and empower by frequent contacts and helps, fulfilling their needs with whatever we can. The more we interact with our network of friends and acquaintances, the more opportunities we encounter, and coincidences triggering ideas about how to get the desired creative ideas.

Have a relaxed attitude, take things easy. We can release more energy and easily recognize opportunities. Stay relaxed and pay attention to what is happening around us; we "discover" something new every day, happenings meaningful to our purpose that encourage us to think further in this direction.

Be open to new experiences in our lives. Break away from routine, e.g., use different ways to work sometimes, dine in different restaurants anytime we eat out, try different ways to perform a routine task, etc.

Spontaneity, being more open to new experiences, often leads to valuable hints delivered by the multidimensional world.

Having our goal in mind, any incidents we come across might reveal an idea that triggers a creative way to achieve it. If not, keep looking and be alert. The more hints we encounter, the more directions there are for us to think about how to fulfill an intent. Hence, we get to the creative idea faster.

Based on the way the multidimensional world functions, below are the four steps to get creative ideas.

Four-step process to get creative ideas

1. *In the gap between thoughts, place an intention to receive a creative idea.* The habit of continuously thinking prevents us from feeling the true Self within. The rare but precious short time between two thoughts is a valuable gap, because it is when we have contact with our inner power. The best timing for placing an intention is during this valuable gap.

2. *Think intensely about fulfilling this intention.* Often, we do not immediately arrive at a way to fulfill it. Intensely think about the intention and expect to receive ideas about ways to fulfill it. Then stop. That means, get out of the way of the multidimensional world for it to function. Let this world,

where ideas travel all over and multicausal effects are generated, take care of the details.

3. *Maximize coincidences as hints from the universe.* When a revealing hint triggers ideas about how to fulfill the intention, follow through. Implement ideas coming up in the form of doable tasks. Each doable task completed moves us closer to the expected creative ideas.

4. *Repeat the first three steps,* if you are not getting the expected creative idea yet. With repetition, we get closer and closer to the expected result. With each repetition, more relevant information is gathered, better insights are obtained, and the more powerful the momentum becomes.

Because of the function of the multidimensional world, we will get the desired creative idea, sooner or later!

Essentially, we are living in the pure consciousness world, which is a field of all possibilities. It attracts, organizes, correlates, and creates everything. So, starting with an intention and constantly think about it, then expect to get the desired creative idea.

True Wealth

The law of attraction and multi causal relationships help achieving creative ideas

Conclusion: Abundance and Fulfillment

We want a life of abundance and fulfillment. Can we achieve both?

Abundance

Imagine we are in the middle of a forest, lost in a snowy winter. It is getting dark, we feel cold, and snow keeps falling more and more! Luckily, we spot a hut not too far away in front of us. Rushing forward and entering the hut, we find a wood stove but no wood around. Safer, but we still tremble because of the cold.

What will we do? Sit in front of the heater trembling and waiting for the heat? We can wait until the morning and freeze to death. Or should we go outside, gather some dry wood, look for a fire match, start the fire, and wait for the heat?

Obviously, we must start the fire. We must do something to get the heat. However, in society most people have the mentality of sitting in front of the heater, trembling and waiting for the heat. They do nothing but expect the heat!

If we don't serve, we won't earn! Our reward matches our service

Conclusion: Abundance and Fulfillment

In society, many people do not do anything helpful to anyone, but they want money, a lot of money. They envy the comfort, happiness, and abundance of others who work hard for what they enjoy.

Be fair to ourselves and to others. If we do not receive any income, realize that we have not done anything useful to anyone. To earn money, we have to do something beneficial to others. We must improve ourselves to have the required skills and expertise to effectively serve others.

After getting the warmth, we happen to discover a copper jar hidden under the bamboo bed in the dark corner of the hut. Curiously, we pull it out, open the lid, and in ecstasy, we see it full of gold coins. How wonderful! The jar has a note on top: "This jar of gold coins belongs to whoever lucky enough to discover it first. It is a magic jar. Each coin spent for self, but not lavishly and/or in a way harming others, will create one replacement coin; each coin spent to help others will create two more."

Extremely excited, what will we do? Of course, we manage to bring the jar home and share the coins with relatives, friends, neighbors, acquaintances, as many people as we can. Spend one coin, share with others one coin. Keep doing it, and we become richer and richer!

The story is a fairy tale but conveys a valuable message for finances and life.

To earn money, we have to do something useful to others around us. If we are earning nothing, very likely we have done nothing helpful to others. If our income is low, we must realize that our contribution to society is not enough. Providing more service to others, we earn more money and deserve it.

This is just half the message. It is about how to achieve **abundance**.

Fulfillment

However, digging further, we realize the other half, reflecting the ecstasy of the story that we all wish to experience. This is for achieving life fulfillment.

Having money, a lot of money, being filthily rich, does not necessarily bring happiness. Many financially very successful people still feel miserable and empty. Some rich and famous people even commit suicide. So, abundance alone is not enough for a meaningful life.

"Being immensely wealthy and feeling deserving it" is

Conclusion: Abundance and Fulfillment

just the beginning of a fulfilling life. We must have a purpose in life. We have to realize we are spiritual beings, taking a physical form to fulfill a life purpose.

To experience fulfillment, we must see the other half of that truth.

It was shown that each of us was born with unique natural talents. When we use our unique talents, we are deeply happy, losing track of time. We need to search for the pressing need of people in society and blend with these talents. If talents and need are perfectly aligned, we experience **fulfillment**.

We must visualize our unique destiny in the cosmic world and diligently act to get there. We not only enjoy fulfillment at the destination but also in the process.

That is how Oprah Winfrey, defying all odds—poverty, racism, and prejudices—lives her life, enjoys her work every day, and becomes a billionaire.

In summary, we can achieve abundance and fulfillment.

www.ingramcontent.com/pod-product-compliance
Lightning Source LLC
Chambersburg PA
CBHW070310230526
45470CB00002B/810

9781977243393